SCHOLASTIC

Follow the Directions... and Learn!

Dozens of Ready-to-Go Pages That Help Kids Learn to Follow Directions—Independently!

BY DINA ANASTASIO

NEW YORK · TORONTO · LONDON · AUCKLAND · SYDNEY
MEXICO CITY · NEW DELHI · HONG KONG · BUENOS AIRES

Teaching Resources

Cover and interior design by Holly Grundon
Cover illustration by Steve Cox
Interior illustration by George Ulrich

ISBN 0-439-40414-2
Copyright © 2004 by Dina Anastasio

7 8 9 10   40   11 10 09 08 07 06

Contents

Introduction

Welcome!

Following directions is a basic life skill. Everyone needs to be able to follow directions independently in order to complete everyday tasks. Directions help us to fill out applications, follow recipes, travel from here to there, complete forms, and assemble parts. And, following directions is crucial to success in the classroom. Children in particular need to follow directions in order to:

- ◎ complete activities correctly
- ◎ work independently
- ◎ complete class assignments and homework
- ◎ play games and sports
- ◎ solve puzzles

Sometimes, difficulty with following directions can hinder an otherwise capable student's performance. Here's the book you need to help children build these important skills all year long, especially those commonly given in the classroom:

- ◎ underlining
- ◎ circling
- ◎ filling in a blank
- ◎ making a check mark
- ◎ drawing
- ◎ numbering
- ◎ following a sequence
- ◎ using a dictionary
- ◎ making a list

Connections to the Standards

The activities in this book support the following language arts standards and benchmarks outlined by the Mid-continent Research for Education and Learning (McRel), a nationally recognized nonprofit organization that collects and synthesizes national and state K–12 standards.

- ⊕ Uses reading skills and strategies to understand a variety of informational texts.

- ⊕ Gives and responds to oral directions.

Source: *Content Knowledge: A Compendium of Standards and Benchmarks for K–12 Education*, 4th Edition (Mid-continent Research for Education and Learning, 2003)

Using These Pages

These reproducible pages can be used anytime—for whole group instruction, small group, individual seatwork or even homework.

◎ Make a copy of the page for each student.

◎ If working with a student individually, sit quietly with him or her. Together, read each direction slowly and carefully. Have the student explain in his or her own words exactly what he or she is being asked to do.

◎ Remind students to write their name and the date at the top of their paper.

◎ Make sure that students understand and complete the first direction before moving on to the next.

◎ Have students check their work before moving on to the next direction.

◎ When the activity is complete, have students reread all the directions, check each detail, and make any necessary changes. For more strategies, see sidebar at right.

For more strategies, see sidebar at right.

If Students Have Trouble

For a variety of reasons, following directions presents a special challenge for some students. In order to follow directions correctly, they must listen, read slowly and carefully, pay attention, and concentrate. Since remembering the sequence of several steps can be confusing, have students take one direction at a time and think about it until they understand exactly what they are being asked to do. You might have them check off each step as it is completed.

To demonstrate the real-life importance of following directions, you might ask students to dictate or write directions for a familiar task, such as making a peanut butter and jelly sandwich. Then, pantomime following their directions, making some obvious mistakes as you go (such as not taking the lid off the jar)!

Supporting Students Who Have Trouble Following Directions

Discuss your concerns with your school's learning specialist to determine if any testing should be recommended.

Provide both written and oral directions.

As much as possible, seat the student away from auditory or visual distraction.

Speak slowly and clearly, using words like *first*, *next*, *then* and *last*.

Avoid asking the student to write and listen simultaneously.

Start with single directions and gradually move to multi-step directions.

Use a highlighter to indicate the numbers of each step.

Stop periodically to ensure the student is on track.

Check yourself to assess the level of vocabulary you are using.

Have a peer act as a model for the struggling student.

Name _____

Date _____

Back to School

Write your name and the date on the lines above.

(1) **Circle** each thing below that you see at your school.

(2) **Draw** the outline of your school in the empty square.

(3) **Color** the school in your picture the same color as your school.

Follow the Directions . . . and Learn!   Scholastic Teaching Resources

My Own Notebook

Write your name and the date on the lines above.

1 **Color** the flowers on this notebook.

2 How old are you? **Write** the number in the triangle.

3 What color is your hair? **Color** the circle that color.

4 What color are your eyes? **Color** the square that color.

5 **Write** your first name in the oval.

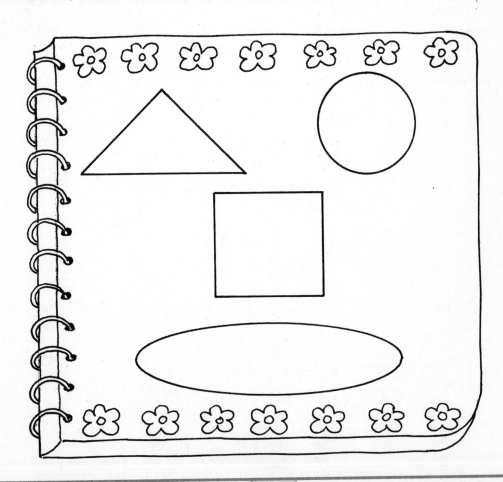

Follow the Directions ... and Learn!   Scholastic Teaching Resources

7

Name _____

Date _____

Grandparents Day
(First Sunday After Labor Day)

Write your name and the date on the lines above.

1. **Color** all the leaves green.

2. **Color** one flower red.

3. **Color** two flowers yellow.

4. **Draw** green stems on all the flowers.

5. **Color** the rest of your card.

Follow the Directions ... and Learn! Scholastic Teaching Resources

First Day of Autumn

Write your name and the date on the lines above.

(1) **Read** each sentence.

(2) **Cross out** the picture word that rhymes with each underlined word.

(3) **Write** that word on the line.

(4) **Read** the poem out loud.

From my window I can <u>see</u>

Yellow leaves up on my _____.

I put away my baseball <u>bat</u>,

And start to wear my autumn _____.

I put away my swimming <u>suits</u>,

And soon I'll wear my winter _____.

Leaves are falling by the <u>lake</u>.

To pick them up I use a _____.

Name _____

Date _____

Apple-Picking Time

Write your name and the date on the lines above.

(1) **Color** two apples red.

(2) **Color** two apples yellow.

(3) **Color** two apples green.

(4) **Draw** a square around the apple at the bottom right corner of this page.

(5) **Write** the color of each apple on the line below it.

_____ _____ _____

_____ _____ _____

Columbus Day

(Second Monday in October)

Write your name and the date on the lines above.

(1) Columbus named his ships the *Niña*, the *Pinta*, and the *Santa Maria*. Decorate your own boat. **Color** the big sail red.

(2) **Color** the small sail blue.

(3) **Color** the medium sail green.

(4) **Choose** a name for your boat. **Write** it on the line.

Follow the Directions ... and Learn!   Scholastic Teaching Resources

11

Name _____

Date _____

United Nations Day

(October 24th)

Write your name and the date on the lines above.

1 The dove is often used as a symbol of peace.
Draw wings on your dove.

2 **Draw** an eye on your dove.

3 **Draw** a tree near the dove.

4 **Give** your dove a name. **Write** it on the line.

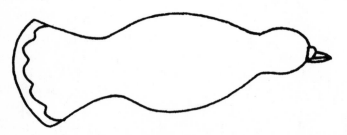

_____

Name _____

Date _____

Halloween Faces

Write your name and the date on the lines above.

(1) **Draw** a happy face on the small pumpkin.

(2) **Draw** a sad face on the medium pumpkin.

(3) **Draw** a scary face on the big pumpkin.

(4) **Color** the pumpkins.

(5) **Underline** your favorite pumpkin.

Name _____

Date _____

Black Cats

Write your name and the date on the lines above.

1 **Draw** a tail on the cat that does not have a tail.

2 **Draw** whiskers on the cat that does not have whiskers.

3 **Draw** ears on the cat that does not have ears.

4 **Color** all the cats black.

Haunted House

Write your name and the date on the lines above.

(1) **Make an X** on each square you can find.

(2) **Color** each triangle black.

(3) **Color** each circle orange.

(4) **Color** the haunted house any color you like.

Happy Halloween

Name _____

Date _____

Autumn Leaves

Write your name and the date on the lines above.

1 **Color** three leaves yellow.

2 **Color** two leaves red.

3 **Color** one leaf brown.

4 **Draw** an orange leaf below.

Name _____

Date _____

Sandwich Day!

(November 3rd)

Write your name and the date on the lines above.

1. **Draw** black stripes on the zebra sandwich.

2. **Color** the fox sandwich red.

3. **Draw** brown spots on the owl sandwich.

4. **Color** the whale sandwich blue.

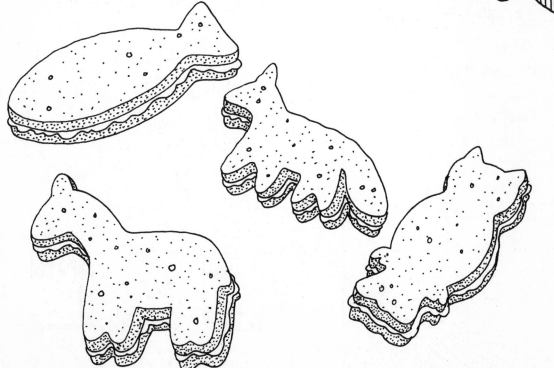

Name _____

Date _____

Election Day

Write your name and the date on the lines above.

1. Let's vote! **Circle** the name of the animal you like best.

2. **Think of** your favorite ice cream. What color is it? **Color** the ice cream that color.

3. **Draw** a line under the book you would most like to read.

My Ballot

1. Dog

   Cat

   Snake

2.

3.

Name _____

Date _____

Ready for Winter

Write your name and the date on the lines above.

1 Birds and squirrels are getting ready for winter.
Underline the acorns.

2 **Circle** the seeds.

3 **Draw** lines connecting the pine cones that are the same shape.

Name _____

Date _____

Thanksgiving Place Cards

Write your name and the date on the lines above.

1 **Circle** the three place cards that are the same.

2 **Underline** the place card that is different.

3 **Write** a family member's name in each rectangle.

4 **Color** the place cards.

Follow the Directions . . . and Learn!   Scholastic Teaching Resources

Thanksgiving Thank-You's

Write your name and the date on the lines above.

(1) **Write** one word to finish the first sentence.

(2) **Write** two words to finish the second sentence.

(3) **Write** three or more words to finish the third sentence.

(4) **Draw** a small picture at the top of your list.

My Thank-You List

I am most thankful for _____.

I am also thankful for _____

_____.

And I give thanks for _____

_____

_____.

Follow the Directions . . . and Learn!   Scholastic Teaching Resources

21

Name _____

Date _____

Flying South for the Winter

Write your name and the date on the lines above.

(1) Draw a bird on the wire. To make the bird's body, **draw** an oval.

(2) **Draw** a round head on the oval body.

(3) **Add** a beak to the round head.

(4) **Draw** wings and feet on the bird.

(5) **Color** all the flying birds blue.
    Color all the birds on the wire red.

Follow the Directions . . . and Learn!   Scholastic Teaching Resources

Bundle Up!

Write your name and the date on the lines above.

① **Color** each thing someone would wear when it's cold.

② **Make an X** on each thing someone would not wear when it's cold.

③ **Write** the word "winter" under each thing someone would wear when it's cold.

_____   _____   _____

_____   _____

Name _____

Date _____

Winter Solstice

(About December 21st)

Write your name and the date on the lines above.

1. **Read** the first two lines of the poem.

2. **Write** the word from the box that rhymes on the line.

3. **Read** the next two lines.

4. **Write** the word that rhymes on the line.

5. **Read** the last two lines of the poem.

6. **Write** the word that rhymes on the line.

Not long ago the sky was bright,

Until I went to bed at _____ .

Now night comes soon.

The sun sinks low.

Where did all the daylight _____ ?

The shortest day of all is here.

It is the shortest of the _____ .

go	year	night

24

In From the Cold

Write your name and the date on the lines above.

1 **Draw** a line from each animal to the place it goes in the winter.

2 Where do you stay warm in the winter? **Draw** your home in the box.

Name _____

Date _____

Happy Holidays!

Write your name and the date on the lines above.

(1) **Write** the name of a friend or family member on each shape.

(2) **Draw** lines between the gifts and tags that are the same shape.

(3) **Color** the matching tags and gifts the same color.

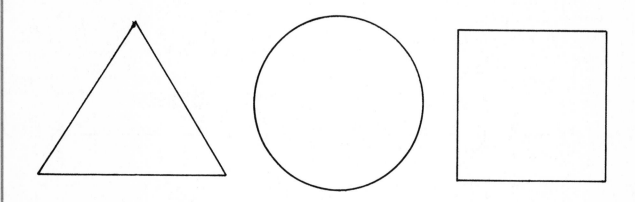

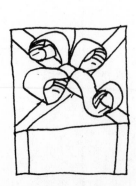

Follow the Directions ... and Learn! Scholastic Teaching Resources

Name _____

December

Date _____

Gift List

Write your name and the date on the lines above.

(**1**) **Write** the name of a friend or family member in the first box.

(**2**) **Write** a gift idea for that person under "Gift Ideas."

(**3**) **Add** more names to the list.

(**4**) **Write** ideas for their gifts in the boxes.

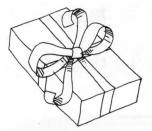

People	Gift Ideas
1.	
2.	
3.	

Name _____

Date _____

Holiday Cookies

Write your name and the date on the lines above.

(1) **Color** the largest cookie pink.

(2) **Add** chocolate chips to two of the cookies.

(3) **Make an X** on the cookie at the bottom left of the page.

(4) **Underline** the cookie at the top right.

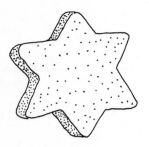
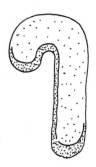
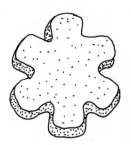

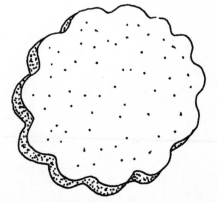

Happy New Year!

Write your name and the date on the lines above.

(1) **Draw** one star on hat 1.

(2) **Draw** two triangles on hat 2.

(3) **Draw** three circles on hat 3.

(4) **Color** all the hats.

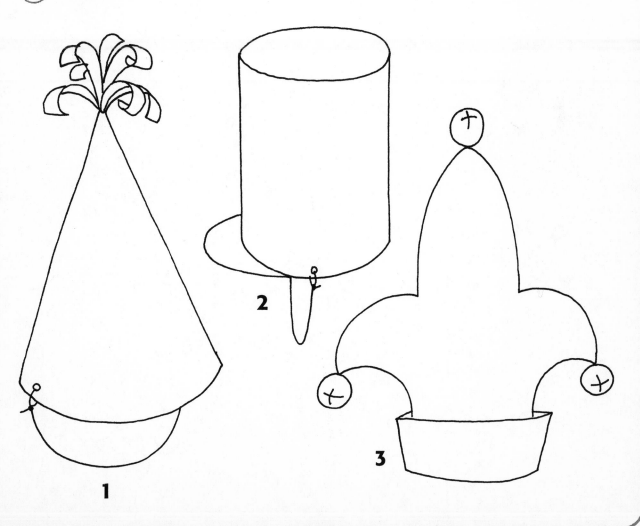

1

2

3

Name _____

Date _____

It's Snowing!

Write your name and the date on the lines above.

1. **Draw** lines connecting snowflakes with the same shape.

2. **Make an X** on each snowflake without a match.

3. **Color** all the snowflakes any colors you like.

Superbowl Sunday

Write your name and the date on the lines above.

(1) **Circle** the trophy you like best.

(2) **Write** your first name on that trophy.

(3) **Color** each trophy.

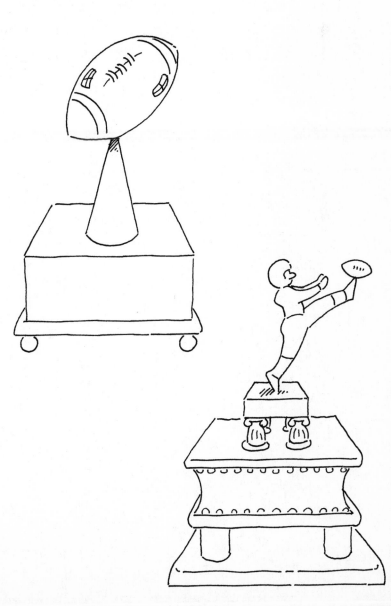

Follow the Directions . . . and Learn!   Scholastic Teaching Resources

31

Name _____

Date _____

Dr. Martin Luther King, Jr., Day

Write your name and the date on the lines above.

① Dr. Martin Luther King, Jr., had a dream. **Write** something you wish for your family on line 1.

② **Write** something you wish for your friends after the number 2.

③ **Write** something you wish for yourself after the number 3.

④ **Draw** a border around your list.

1. _____

_____

2. _____

_____

3. _____

_____

Snowballs!

Write your name and the date on the lines above.

(**1**) **Draw** lines connecting the snowballs that are about the same size.

(**2**) **Color** the small snowballs blue.

(**3**) **Color** the medium snowballs red.

(**4**) **Color** the large snowballs green.

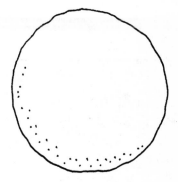
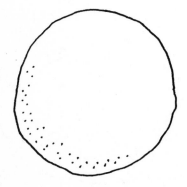
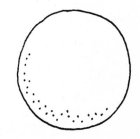
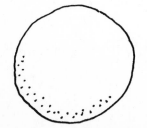

Name _____

Date _____

Winter Changes

Write your name and the date on the lines above.

(1) The white-tailed jack rabbit changes color in the winter so it can hide in the snow. **Color** the ears of the winter rabbit to match the autumn rabbit.

(2) **Color** the body and head of the autumn rabbit light brown. Do not color the tail.

(3) **Color** the eyes of each rabbit yellow.

Autumn

Winter

Follow the Directions ... and Learn!   Scholastic Teaching Resources

Name _____

Date _____

February Calendar

Write your name and the date on the lines above.

① **Color** the presidents' birthdays blue.

② **Color** all the weekend days yellow.

③ **Make an X** on today's date.

④ **Draw** a pet on February 21st.

February						
Sunday	**Monday**	**Tuesday**	**Wednesday**	**Thursday**	**Friday**	**Saturday**
1	2 Groundhog Day	3	4	5	6	7
8	9	10	11	12 Lincoln's Birthday	13	14 Valentine's Day
15	16	17	18	19	20	21 Pet Day
22 Washington's Birthday	23	24	25	26	27	28

Name _____

Date _____

Groundhog Day
(February 2nd)

Write your name and the date on the lines above.

① **Color** the groundhog.

② **Draw** the groundhog's shadow behind him.

③ **Draw** a straight line from the groundhog to his hole.

Be My Valentine!

(February 14th)

Write your name and the date on the lines above.

1. **Write** the first name of a friend or family member next to the word TO on each valentine.

2. **Write** your first name next to the word FROM in each valentine.

3. **Draw** lines connecting the valentines with exactly the same border.

4. **Color** all the valentines.

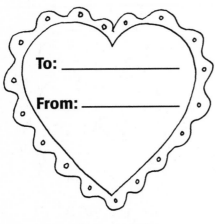

Name _____

Date _____

Presidential Birthdays

Write your name and the date on the lines above.

(1) **Write** *Washington* under the president on the left and *Lincoln* under the president on the right.

(2) **Color** both presidents.

(3) **Draw** a hat on Abraham Lincoln.

_____   _____

Build a Snowman

Write your name and the date on the lines above.

(**1**) **Draw** a face on the top circle.

(**2**) **Draw** stick arms on your snowman.

(**3**) **Draw** three black buttons on the middle circle.

(**4**) **Draw** a red hat on your snowman.

Name _____

Date _____

Chinese New Year Dragon

Write your name and the date on the lines above.

1 **Color** the dragon red.

2 **Choose** a name for your dragon and **write** it on the line.

3 On the back of this sheet, **write** a sentence telling why you would or would not want a dragon as a pet.

4 **Draw** a red border around your dragon.

_____

Follow the Directions ... and Learn! Scholastic Teaching Resources

Saint Patrick's Day

Write your name and the date on the lines above.

1 **Color** four clovers light green and four dark green.

2 **Make an X** on the four-leaf clover.

3 **Circle** the smallest clover.

4 **Add** one more four-leaf clover.

Name _____

Date _____

Luck of the Irish

Write your name and the date on the lines above.

1. **Color** your good luck charm green.

2. **Make** your charm look like a flower. **Draw** flower petals around the outside of your charm.

3. **Color** the ribbon yellow.

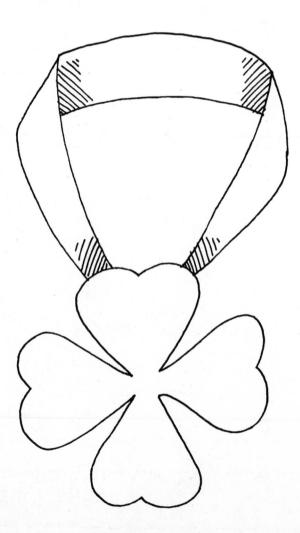

Reading Month

Write your name and the date on the lines above.

(**1**) **Make up** a title for a book. **Write** it in the rectangle.

(**2**) **Draw** a cover picture on your book.

(**3**) **Write** your first and last name on the line.

by _____

Name _____

Date _____

Spring Bookmarks

Write your name and the date on the lines above.

1 **Color** all the shorter tulips the same color.

2 **Color** all the taller tulips different colors.

3 **Draw** stems on all the little flowers at the bottom of each bookmark.

4 **Cut out** your bookmarks and give them to friends or family.

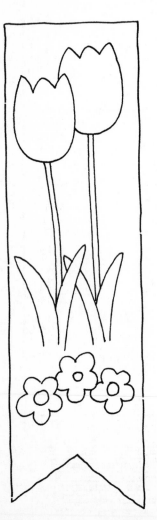 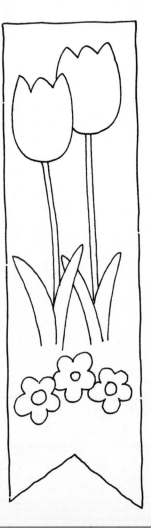 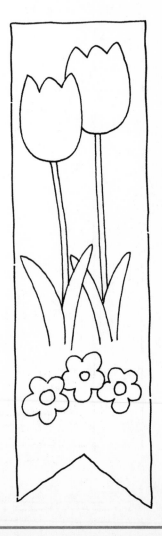

Follow the Directions ... and Learn!   Scholastic Teaching Resources

March Flowers

Write your name and the date on the lines above.

① Crocuses are March flowers. **Circle** each crocus that has not opened yet.

② **Color** the stems of the open crocuses green.

③ **Color** two open crocuses blue.

④ **Color** two open crocuses yellow.

Name _____

Date _____

Flying North

Write your name and the date on the lines above.

① **Circle** all the butterflies that look like this .

② **Draw** lines connecting the butterflies that match.

③ **Make an X** on the butterfly that does not have a match.

④ **Color** all the butterflies.

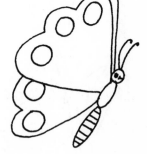

April Fools Day

Write your name and the date on the lines above.

(1) **Circle** each thing in the sky that is silly.

(2) **Make an X** on the thing in the water that is silly.

(3) **Underline** each thing on the ground that is silly.

Follow the Directions ... and Learn!   Scholastic Teaching Resources

47

Name _____

Date _____

Easter Egg Hunt

Write your name and the date on the lines above.

1 **Draw** eyes, a nose, and a mouth on each egg.

2 **Draw** a hat on the little egg.

3 **Draw** a moustache on the medium egg.

4 **Draw** hair on the large egg.

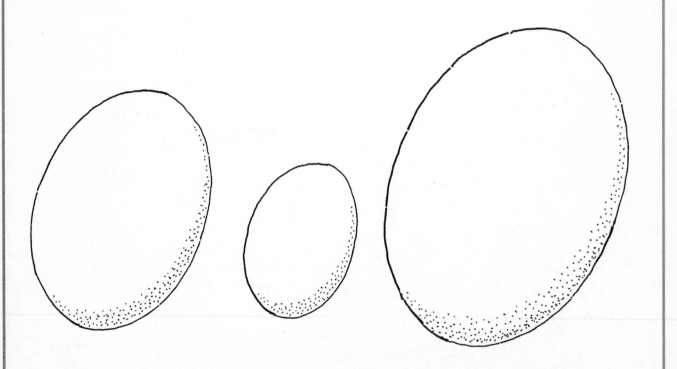

Earth Day

Write your name and the date on the lines above.

(1) **Color** the United States green.

(2) **Color** the oceans blue.

(3) **Make an X** to show the place you live.

CANADA

UNITED STATES

ATLANTIC
OCEAN

PACIFIC
OCEAN

Name _____

Date _____

Recycle It!

Write your name and the date on the lines above.

(1) **Draw** three pencils in the can.

(2) **Draw** a flower in the water bottle.

(3) **Write** "Happy Birthday" on the paper bag.

(4) **Decorate** the bag.

April Showers

Write your name and the date on the lines above.

(**1**) **Color** the stripe with a 1 red.

(**2**) **Color** the stripe with a 2 green.

(**3**) **Color** the stripe with a 3 yellow.

(**4**) **Color** the stripes with 4s blue.

(**5**) **Draw** a handle on your umbrella. **Draw** yourself under the umbrella.

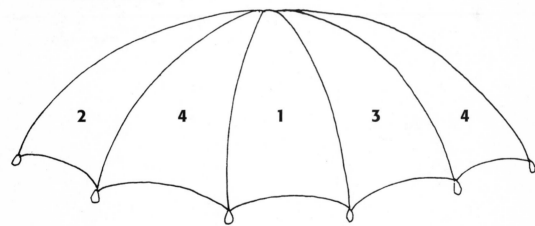

Follow the Directions ... and Learn!   Scholastic Teaching Resources

51

Name _____

Date _____

Arbor Day

(Around April 22nd)

Write your name and the date on the lines above.

(1) **Place** the palm of your hand on this page.

(2) **Spread** out your fingers so they look like branches.

(3) **Trace** around your fingers.

(4) **Draw** a tree trunk below your branches.

(5) **Draw** three leaves on each branch.

Follow the Directions . . . and Learn! Scholastic Teaching Resources

Name _____

Date _____

May Day

Write your name and the date on the lines above.

1 **Color** two streamers red.

2 **Color** two streamers yellow.

3 **Color** two streamers green.

4 **Color** the maypole blue and purple.

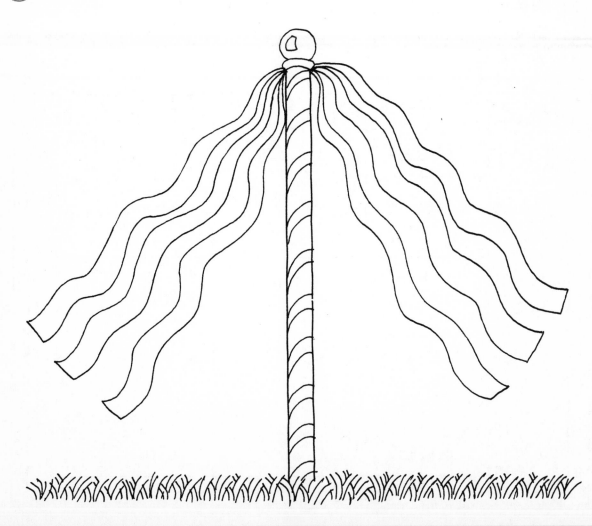

Name _____

Date _____

Happy Teacher's Day!

Write your name and the date on the lines above.

(1) **Write** your teacher's name in the rectangle on the card.

(2) **Write** your name on the line.

(3) **Draw** two May flowers on the card.

(4) **Draw** a sun on the card.

(5) **Color** your card.

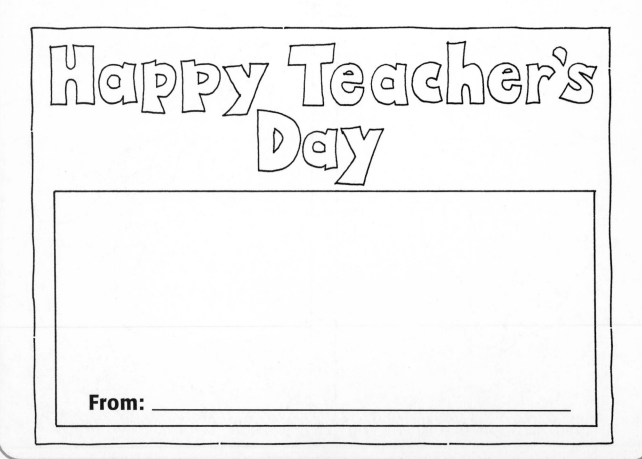

From: _____

May Flowers

Write your name and the date on the lines above.

(1) **Make an X** on the flower with nine petals.

(2) **Circle** the two flowers that are the same.

(3) **Color** the smaller flowers pink and orange.

(4) **Color** the bigger flowers yellow and purple.

Name _____

Date _____

Spring Babies

Write your name and the date on the lines above.

1. **Draw** a line from each mother animal to her baby.

2. **Label** each mother and baby. Use the words in the box.

_____

_____

_____

_____

_____

_____

| goat | kid | elephant | calf | horse | foal |

Follow the Directions … and Learn! Scholastic Teaching Resources

It's Mother's Day!

Write your name and the date on the lines above.

(1) **Draw** a red design at the top of this Mother's Day card.

(2) **Draw** four hearts on your card.

(3) **Color** two hearts pink and two hearts yellow.

(4) **Write** your name on the line.

From: _____

Name _____

Date _____

Breakfast in Bed

Write your name and the date on the lines above.

(1) **Make a check mark** (✓) next to each food your mother likes.

(2) **Circle** each food that you like.

(3) **Make an X** on the foods that are shown in twos.

Name _____

Date _____

Father's Day

Write your name and the date on the lines above.

① **Read** the song out loud, two lines at a time.

② **Find** each rhyming word in the word box.

③ **Write** each rhyming word on the line.

④ **Sing** the song to the tune of "Twinkle, Twinkle Little Star."

Happy Father's Day to Dad

I'll be good. I won't be _____.

I'll be quiet when you're sick.

I will never hit or _____.

I won't yell or shout or moan,

When you're talking on the _____.

Let's play the games you want to play!

It's Father's Day! It's Father's _____!

kick	phone	Day	bad

Name _____

Date _____

Flag Day

(June 14th)

Write your name and the date on the lines above.

1. **Color** every other stripe red.

2. **Color** the square blue. Do not color in the stars.

3. **Count** all the stripes. **Write** the number next to them.

4. **Count** all the stars. **Write** the number next to them.

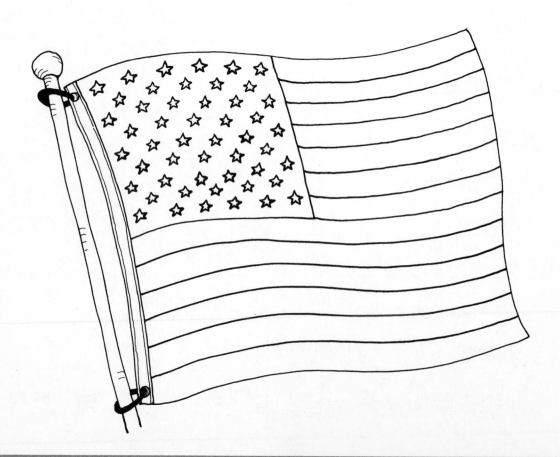

Name _____

Date _____

Summer Reading List

Write your name and the date on the lines above.

(1) **Make a check mark** (✓) after the book you would most like to read in each row.

(2) **Write** the title of a book you recently read here: _____.

(3) **Color** the book covers on this page any colors you like.

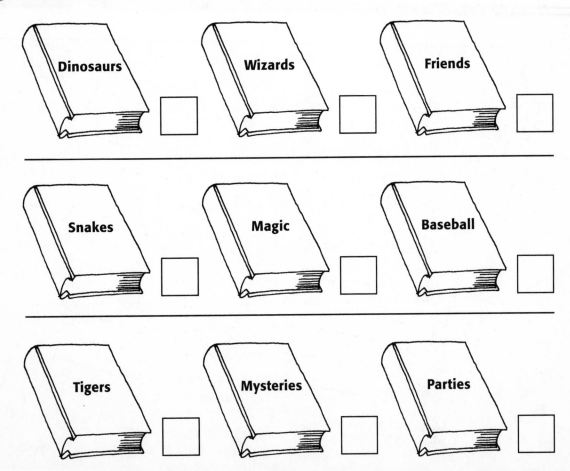

Name _____

Date _____

Hello, Summer!

Write your name and the date on the lines above.

(1) **Read** each sentence aloud.

(2) **Circle** the picture and word that fits in each blank.

(3) **Write** the picture words on the lines.

sun

Winter's over. Spring is done.

Time to play out in the _____.

Summer's here. Let's stay up late.

The sun won't set till after _____.

Goodbye jackets. Goodbye school.

Hello swimsuits. Hello _____.

Hello berries, corn, and heat.

Hello nothing on my _____.

pool

feet

8
eight

Follow the Directions . . . and Learn!   Scholastic Teaching Resources

Name _____

Date _____

Fourth of July

Write your name and the date on the lines above.

(1) **Circle** the five horns that are the same.

(2) **Make an X** on the horn that is different from all the rest.

(3) **Color** all the horns any colors you like.

Name _____

Date _____

Summer Sandcastle

Write your name and the date on the lines above.

① **Draw** two sticks on top of your castle.

② **Draw** four round windows on your castle.

③ **Draw** a sun somewhere on this page.

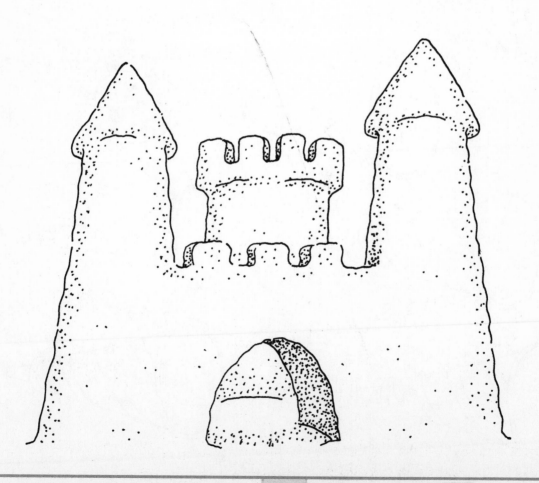

Follow the Directions . . . and Learn!   Scholastic Teaching Resources